D1525163

Newsmakers™

Hamid Karzai

**President of
Afghanistan**

Philip Wolny

ROSEN
PUBLISHING®

New York

Published in 2008 by The Rosen Publishing Group, Inc.
29 East 21st Street, New York, NY 10010

First Edition

Library of Congress Cataloging-in-Publication Data

Wolny, Philip.
Hamid Karzai : president of Afghanistan / Philip Wolny.—1st ed.
    p. cm.—(Newsmakers)
Includes bibliographical references and index.
ISBN-13: 978-1-4042-1902-1
ISBN-10: 1-4042-1902-1
1. Karzai, Hamid, 1957—Juvenile literature. 2. Presidents—
Afghanistan—Biography—Juvenile literature.
I. Title.
DS371.43.K37W66 2007
958.104'7092—dc22
[B]
                                                                2006101205

Manufactured in the United States of America

On the cover: Foreground: Hamid Karzai in 2006. Background: Afghan Guard at the Presidential Palace in 2006.

CONTENTS

INTRODUCTION

On September 16, 2004, a missile barely missed the helicopter transporting President Hamid Karzai to a school opening in Gardez, the capital town of Paktia province in southeastern Afghanistan. Had he been killed, the Taliban, the former Islamic fundamentalist rulers of this war-plagued central Asian nation, would have scored a major blow against their enemies.

This was not the first assassination attempt against Karzai. Two years earlier, a man disguised as a member of the then newly formed Afghan

Hamid Karzai declares victory in Afghanistan's election during a speech at the Presidential Palace in Kabul, Afghanistan, on November 4, 2005.

National Army (ANA) opened fire in Karzai's direction while the president was visiting his birthplace of Kandahar, which is now a Taliban hotspot. The man was actually one of Karzai's appointed bodyguards that day. The governor of Kandahar was wounded and an American special operations officer was killed when Karzai's other bodyguards shot back. That the assassin missed his target was a close call for Karzai, whose own father was assassinated in Pakistan years earlier, most likely by members of the Taliban or their allies. But it was almost just another day's work for Karzai, who has been through conflict, compromise, and heartache, and now works fourteen-hour days trying to steer his country in what he believes is the right direction.

Karzai is a man seemingly in danger from all sides. Even in areas considered to be more secure, like Afghanistan's capital, Kabul, the reach of the Taliban and other antigovernment forces makes life dangerous. Critics have scoffed that Karzai is not really the president of Afghanistan, but the "Mayor of Kabul." This sarcastic nickname refers to his lack of power outside of the capital. It is also a biting criticism of the fact that he seldom ventures out of his compound for fear of assassination.

These are the perils facing the president of a nation that is struggling to find itself after the latest in a long history of foreign invasions. In 2001, responding to the September 11 terrorist attacks on American soil that claimed more than 3,000 lives, the United States went to war against Afghanistan—specifically the Taliban—enlisting the help of the Northern Alliance, the Taliban's longtime enemy, in unseating the government. It was an invasion marked by heavy bombing from the air and many small revolts throughout the country. Karzai provided invaluable help in the war effort.

Hamid Karzai is a complex man leading a complex country. He is a proud member of Afghanistan's complex majority who connects easily with the members of its various ethnic minorities. A diplomatic, soft-spoken but shrewd politician, he leads a nation that is now one of the most important fronts in the international war on terrorism. He is also the first democratically elected leader in a nation that has changed hands more often than some observers can count.

With his education, history, diplomatic skills, and even his fashion sense, Karzai cuts an impressive figure on the international stage. To many Afghans, however, he is a controversial figure. On one hand, he is a hero of both the Afghan struggle against Soviet occupation in the 1980s and the war that deposed the Taliban.

On the other, he is a man who cannot say no to both the warlords that still exert power in his country and to the United States and other powerful allies. Karzai is at times stuck between a rock and a hard place when it comes to leading Afghanistan.

For his supporters at home and abroad—especially in the United States—the battle Karzai wages is not only for Afghanistan, but also for the safety of the world itself. American president George W. Bush told Karzai during a White House press conference on May 23, 2005, "Your leadership has been strong, and it's in our interests that Afghanistan remains free. Afghanistan is no longer a safe haven for terrorists. Afghanistan is a key partner in the global war on terror."

Karzai's success or failure will undoubtedly affect the outcome of the war on terror. Whether in Madrid, Spain, or in Peoria, Illinois, the people of the world look to his work with great concern. But Afghanistan faces other challenges, too. Will Karzai be able to bring a nation destroyed by war into the twenty-first century, fixing its shattered infrastructure, alleviating its poverty, and nurturing its fragile democracy? For many, Hamid Karzai—Afghan politician, leader, statesman—remains the country's greatest hope.

CHAPTER ONE

THE EARLY YEARS

Hamid Karzai was born in Kandahar on December 24, 1957, during the reign of Mohammad Zahir Shah, Afghanistan's last king. Zahir Shah had been an important leader who helped to modernize Afghanistan politically and economically by establishing the country's first-ever legislature and supporting education for women, among other reforms.

Hamid's father, Abdul Ahad Karzai, was the head of the influential Popalzai clan and served as a member of the Afghan Parliament. The Popalzai were among the strongest supporters of the king. They were Pashtuns, Afghanistan's largest ethnic group.

Young Hamid began his schooling in Kandahar, and then moved with his father to Kabul, Afghanistan's capital, where he finished his secondary education at Habibia High School. In June 2002, Karzai told an audience at the

Academy of Achievement in Dublin, Ireland, about his childhood: "By Afghan standards, we were well off . . . In Kabul, of course, life was very good. We had as much access to good music and movies—which, at that age, people really want—as any kid would have in Europe or America, and a good education, a fairly good life."

KARZAI THE STUDENT

As a student, Karzai remembers himself to have been serious and quiet. As he grew older, he was in part influenced by his father's leadership role in the national and tribal government. He told the Academy of Achievement, "I partially wanted to do the kind of parliamentary stuff that my father was doing, and I was also interested in the University of Kabul, which at that time was a very prestigious institution. The professors there were very well-respected and they had very nice lives. The environment of the university was so enchanting. That was the kind of life I wanted." Exposed to the university through his father's contacts, he would later experience academia firsthand while studying in Simla, India.

Among Hamid's favorite subjects in school were science, especially chemistry, and Charles Darwin's theory of evolution. A high school chemistry teacher once became very angry with him for knowing things that the teacher didn't. In addition to Afghan writers, Hamid also enjoyed Russian writers such as Anton Chekhov and Fyodor Dostoevsky, and British author Charles Dickens.

LEADERSHIP AND NONVIOLENCE

Hamid's heroes during his younger years also reflect a desire for justice and strong leadership: Indian leader Mahatma Gandhi, South African dissident and longtime prisoner Nelson Mandela, and American civil rights leader Martin Luther

Hamid Karzai has cited Mahatma Gandhi, leader of the Indian independence movement, as an influence and inspiration for his philosophy of nonviolence.

King Jr. Hamid was especially impressed by Gandhi, telling the Academy of Achievement, "I'm most affected by Gandhi. The struggle for independence of his country and the way he did it through peaceful means: non-violence, and the tolerance that he preached, and the way he respected mankind as a whole, and his self-restraint. A wonderful human being."

Hamid also admired his father greatly, whom he saw much in the same light as his other heroes. The son particularly approved of "his parliamentary elections, his conduct with the tribes. We are a tribal people, and the way his house would be open to people all the time was something that came automatically. And his love for peace. He hated violence. That was something that I admired in him a lot. He hated guns very much." It was the openness to all groups that would be a big part of Karzai's approach to running Afghanistan years later.

KARZAI: THE COLLEGE YEARS

From 1976 to 1982, Hamid Karzai was a student at Himachal University in Simla, in the state of

Himachal Pradesh, India. India was a bit of a
culture shock for Hamid Karzai. He had grown
up wealthy and exposed to many Western and
other foreign influences. But, he had little contact
with people of other cultures as a child. As a
result, he was shy when he first met people during
his university life. "I recognized when I went to
India, when I mixed up with other students there,
that I was . . . very, very reserved, and that was a
handicap." He noted, however, that this character
trait helped him to defer to others and develop
the sensitivity necessary for a leader dealing
with others.

AFGHANISTAN IN A
TIME OF CHANGE

As Karzai grew to adulthood, his country was
changing. Mohammad Zahir Shah had ruled over
the country for forty peaceful years. Afghanistan
had experienced violence before then. Having,
throughout the course of its history, been
invaded by Arabs, Mongols, and the British, the
nation has had a violent past. But in 1973, Zahir
Shah's brother-in-law, Sardar Mohammed Daoud

Mohammad Zahir Shah, ex-king of Afghanistan, is shown here in Rome in September 2001. Before the Loya Jirga picked Karzai, some Afghans pushed for Zahir Shah's return to the throne.

Khan, overthrew the king in a bloodless coup, or takeover.

From then on, Daoud Khan led the Republic of Afghanistan as president. However, there was little democracy allowed in the country at this time. The Loya Jirga, the traditional grand council that makes important decisions in Afghanistan, still functioned, but its leaders were mostly appointed, and not elected. In 1977, the Loya Jirga approved Daoud Khan's constitution, and he established the National Revolutionary Party as Afghanistan's only political party.

Also at this time, Islamic fundamentalism was growing in Afghanistan and around the world. (Islamic fundamentalists believe that they must spread the word of Islam, at times violently if necessary, and the culture and government of traditionally Muslim nations should adhere strictly to its rule.) Daoud Khan used the military to defeat some of these extremists, who fled, mainly to Pakistan.

THE SOVIET INVASION

In April 1977, Daoud Khan met with the leader of the Soviet Union, Leonid Brezhnev, to discuss Afghani-Soviet relations. He was concerned about Soviet influence, particularly through Afghanistan's two Communist parties, Parcham and Khalq. The following year, fearing the growing power of the Communists in his country, Daoud Khan issued arrest orders for several of the

parties' leaders. Many escaped. However, one of
them, Hafizullah Amin, ordered a coup while
under house arrest.

On April 27, rebels began fighting Daoud
Khan's forces near Kabul International Airport.
The revolt quickly spread. On April 28, Daoud
Khan was killed along with most of his family at
the Presidential Palace in Kabul. The rebels
claimed publicly that he had "resigned for health
reasons." Forces opposing the rebels soon
started resisting their new Communist rulers.
In response, late December, 1979, the Soviet
Union invaded Afghanistan to "save" the
Communist government there.

KARZAI AND THE SOVIET INVASION

Hamid Karzai was still studying in Simla, India,
at the time. He saw the news on the front page
of the daily newspapers. He was emotionally
crushed. He later explained to the Academy of
Achievement, "My feeling at that moment suddenly
was of a loss. I felt smaller. Much, much smaller
than I felt before that when I was walking to my

The Soviet Union invaded Afghanistan in 1979 to support the besieged Communist government there. In this photo, a Red Army tank rides through the Afghan countryside in December 1979.

college. I heard people talk about this invasion and suddenly I felt a loss of identity."

Soon after, Karzai took a bus about 3,000 kilometers (about 1,864 miles) to the eastern border of Afghanistan (with Pakistan). It was here that he saw the first of the estimated five million Afghans eventually displaced by the invasion and later civil war. Many Afghans fled to neighboring Iran and Pakistan, with over three million settling in the latter.

"HELP ME GO BACK HOME"

It was the resilience of the people that impressed Karzai the most. For example, as he told the Academy of Achievement: "I had some money with me. It was my stipend money that my mother had sent me. I handed out some of that money to one of my fellow Afghans who was a refugee. He was insulted. He said, 'What do you think of me?' I said, 'I'm trying to help.' He said, 'No. Don't help by handing me some money. If you really want to help, you help the whole of Afghanistan. Help me go back home.'"

The invasion by the Soviets sparked a civil war that would involve the major powers of the day: the Soviet Union and the United States. Many of the Afghan exiles in Pakistan worked to overthrow the Soviet-supported government in their native land. According to a memoir by Robert Gates, the director of the United States'

Central Intelligence Agency (CIA) at the time, the United States started helping anti-Communist forces as early as six months before the invasion. In July 1979, U.S. president Jimmy Carter authorized the use of covert propaganda by the CIA to oppose the Afghan Communists and their Soviet allies.

The Soviets were unprepared for fighting in a place such as Afghanistan. Their military had been trained to fight large armies on battlefields. Instead, they were fighting loose groups of rebels who used guerilla tactics. In guerilla warfare, small groups fight wherever they can, often using surprise attacks. There is no set battlefield. The mountains and desert climate of Afghanistan also proved difficult for Soviet forces. They were unused to fighting in the harsh environment of Afghanistan.

A LIFE IN EXILE

Karzai's own family suffered during and after the invasion. As he told the Academy of Achievement, "My father was taken to prison. A lot of our relatives were killed by the Communists and the Soviets in a brutal way. So were the relatives and fathers of a lot of other Afghan children at that time. It was the same all over the country. It was a horrible thing."

Much of Karzai's family eventually fled to Quetta, Pakistan. It was there that they, along with many Afghan exiles, actively worked against the Soviets. They helped raise money to support the fighters struggling against the Soviets. These fighters were called mujahideen, translated as "strugglers" or "holy warriors."

The United States secretly funded the Afghan rebels. It did this with middlemen, most often members of Pakistan's secret police, the Inter-Services Intelligence (ISI). The United States used the Pakistanis to hide the fact that it was helping Afghans and their allies against the Soviets. This was because the United States did not officially declare war on the Soviet Union, which could have led to worldwide disaster.

AFGHAN ARABS

Many of the fighters who volunteered to fight the Soviets were not natives of Afghanistan.

Thousands of volunteers from other Muslim, and mainly Arab, nations, flooded into the country to join the civil war. Some people have named them the Afghan Arabs. Many Afghans were patriots who were simply fighting an invasion by the Soviets. The so-called Afghan Arabs saw it as their duty as Muslims to defeat Communism. They saw Communism as an atheist, and therefore anti-Muslim, movement.

One of them was a man who was not primarily a fighter, but a financier of the movement. The Saudi billionaire businessman Osama bin Laden funneled great amounts of money to the mujahideen during the 1980s. He came from a wealthy family but had earned more money as the owner of several large construction businesses.

CHAPTER TWO

KARZAI AT WAR

In the 1980s, Hamid Karzai's beloved Afghanistan was at war. On one side were the mujahideen and their secret supporters, the United States and Pakistan. On the other was the Afghan government and the Soviet military.

It was long before the world ever heard of Al Qaeda or the Taliban. Among the mujahideen fighting the guerilla war in Afghanistan were the first of what the world would later know as the Taliban. Karzai met many of these fighters during his work against the Soviets.

Many of the mujahideen who also fought against the Soviets would later oppose the Taliban as well. When Karzai later returned to Afghanistan, the seeds planted during this time would bloom. A lifetime of struggling for

Anti-Soviet mujahideen are stationed at an antiaircraft unit in Kunar, eastern Afghanistan, during the Afghan civil war that ravaged the nation in the 1980s.

Afghanistan would make Karzai well known to those whose support he needed.

KARZAI: FREEDOM FIGHTER BEHIND THE SCENES

The fight against the Soviets was long and hard. Most sources admit that Karzai never physically fought in any battles during this time. Rather, he acted as an unofficial diplomat, traveling the world to convince the international community to help the Afghan rebel cause. Still, he was in some danger, and his family was, too. Anyone speaking out against the Soviet-supported government had to fear for their safety. It was a war zone, after all; either the Soviets or their Afghan supporters would punish those against them.

The Soviet battle to keep Afghanistan Communist was a losing one. The land and climate were harsh. The Soviets had better weapons and fearsome helicopters, but the will of a people to be free of outside occupation was stronger. The secret support of the United States and Pakistani intelligence services was also important.

With American weapons and money for supplies, the mujahideen wore down the Soviets.

The Soviets lost about 14,453 soldiers in the fight against the mujahideen, according to Red Army (Soviet) statistics. The exact amount of Afghan soldiers and civilians, and other mujahideen from other countries, is unknown. According to Amnesty International, however, it is estimated that more than one million Afghan civilians perished.

THE WAR ENDS, A NEW ONE BEGINS

Karzai and many other Afghans were thrilled when the Soviets finally withdrew on February 15, 1989. Many Afghans stuck in Pakistan, Iran, and other places around the world hoped to come home. Karzai was among them.

Without the support of the Soviets to hold the country together, things quickly fell apart. The government of Mohammed Najibullah, the Communist leader at the time, soon fell apart. Many of the old rivalries between warlords and ethnic groups arose again. Many of those who had fought the Soviets together now turned on each other.

The situation soon became terrible. Power changed hands almost daily, and lawlessness was the rule rather than the exception. The soldiers of the warlords, many of them now experienced in fighting the Soviets, killed each other. Because there was no such thing as a police force or common government, terrible crimes went unpunished. The only law seemed to be revenge. The population suffered greatly. Rape and robbery became common. Afghans could not travel because they were in danger of being robbed and killed. Burhanuddin Rabbani was the official leader of Afghanistan at this time, but in reality he controlled only the capital city of Kabul.

Karzai told the Academy of Achievement: "When the country went to anarchy. . . one of these [warlords] came to me and said, 'Hamid, we were friends when we were fighting the Soviet Union . . . Look at this country. What happened to this country? War everywhere, anarchy, looting, insults to women, insults to the sovereignty of this country. Can we do something about it?'"

Karzai responded that he wasn't sure how. The warlord suggested that those who were angered by the crime, killing, and other problems brought by the civil war should get together and put a stop to it. Karzai later said, "This is how the process of the Taliban began. Now, I did not know at that stage that there were other forces behind [it], with other intentions."

OUTSIDERS TAKE OVER

The other forces that Karzai was talking about were some of the same allies that had helped fight the Soviets: the Pakistani ISI and the foreign mujahideen, or Afghan Arabs. Islamic fundamentalism had been growing for years and would become a powerful movement in the 1980s and a threat to world security in the 1990s. Many Afghans in Pakistan had become close with radical Pakistanis. Madrassas, or religious schools teaching a very strict form of Islam, sprang up all over Pakistan, especially in the areas just over the border from Afghanistan. Madrassas taught boys from a young age well into adulthood. These schools graduated many fundamentalists who were ready to work against Western influence in Afghanistan.

THE STUDENTS TAKE ACTION

The movement came to be known as the Taliban, from the Arabic word *talib*, which means "a seeker of knowledge" or "student." "Taliban" referred to the students of these madrassas.

Karzai admitted that many of those who supported the Taliban, including himself, had good intentions. The Taliban was the only one who was ready to stand up to the warlordism destroying the country. The choice between the warlords and the Taliban was clear. Many people welcomed the Taliban. They believed the Taliban would clean up the country and restore order.

The Taliban and its supporters wanted more than order and safety. They also wanted to unite Afghanistan under strict Islamic rule. The foreign Arab mujahideen who made the country their new home were among the supporters. Karzai said of the Taliban to the Academy of Achievement, "Very soon, they were taken over by foreigners, by the Pakistanis, by the Arab elements, by radical Muslims . . . the movement was completely sabotaged."

Hamid Karzai *(far right)* speaks to the new leader of Afghanistan, President Sibghatullah Mojaddedi, after the latter's takeover of power from the Communist regime in 1992.

RETURN AND REALIZATION

Karzai had returned to Afghanistan in 1992. He even worked as deputy foreign minister under the weak, unsteady government of Burhanuddin Rabbani. He saw within eight months or so that the honest and patriotic Afghans within the Taliban were being replaced by fundamentalists.

Karzai was scared by this, but he hoped that the movement could be saved. He continued to supply the Taliban with help. "I gave them the money I had, and they were given money from outside," he told the Academy of Achievement. Soon, he realized that the good members of the Taliban were getting poorer, and the corrupt ones wealthier.

BIN LADEN AND THE TALIBAN

In 1996, Osama bin Laden came to Afghanistan. Karzai did not know who he was, exactly, but he had heard of him. Karzai spoke to a pilot in Afghanistan who claimed he had flown bin Laden to visit Mullah Omar. Omar was an

Shown here is Taliban leader Mullah Omar, a close ally of Osama bin Laden's. Omar remains among the most wanted men in the world.

ex-mujahideen and one of the most powerful members of the Taliban. The pilot said that bin Laden had given Omar briefcases full of money.

By this time, the Taliban had taken power in most of Afghanistan. Only the most northern provinces were free. These were controlled by the warlords who opposed the Taliban, many of them also veteran mujahideen. Collectively, these warlords were known as the Northern Alliance. The Taliban was mainly Pashtuns, but the Northern Alliance was made up of the nation's ethnic minorities: Tajiks, Uzbeks, and Hayaras, among others.

Burqa-clad women wait behind an iron fence for relief from an aid agency on November 19, 2001, hoping to procure items they need to survive through the harsh Afghan winter.

AN ALLY NO MORE

Karzai saw the Taliban creating a nation that made him more and more uneasy. It was banning women from working or receiving an education. It imposed harsh laws for minor crimes. For example, someone stealing a loaf of bread had his hand cut off. A woman who was unfaithful to her husband or anyone who spoke out against Islam risked the death penalty.

For Karzai, this was completely unlike the Afghanistan he had grown up in. Karzai traveled abroad at this time, trying to warn Western leaders about the Taliban. The Europeans and Americans he met with thought he was over-reacting. He said, "Very few people believed me. They said… 'You are saying this because they are not the type of people you are… You speak English, you are educated, so you don't represent Afghanistan. The Taliban do represent Afghanistan.'" This idea that Karzai is somehow different from the common Afghan lingers among his critics even today.

Eventually, Karzai decided to abandon the Taliban and work against it. He fled to Pakistan. This decision would have tragic consequences.

A FAMILY TRAGEDY

Karzai and those who believed as he did were on their own, more or less. Many of his family members opposed the Taliban alongside him. Karzai's father worked against the Taliban from safer ground: the city of Quetta in Pakistan.

However, there were many pro-Taliban supporters in Pakistan. On July 14, 1999, Karzai's father was coming back from evening prayers. An assassin crept up behind him and shot him. Karzai says his father was killed because he was becoming a threat to the Taliban. He had outspokenly called for a Loya Jirga (traditional Afghan national council) to get rid of the Taliban. The death of his father made Karzai angry and sad. But he made a decision to stand up to the Taliban. He decided to return to Afghanistan with his father's body.

THE ROAD TO KANDAHAR

When Karzai told everyone he was taking his father's body back to Kandahar, his father's birthplace, most of them thought he was crazy. He recalled, "Lots of people came to me and said, 'Don't do that. You will go into Afghanistan and the Taliban will arrest you.'" He replied,

"No. I want to go, and if they have the guts, let them arrest me."

So, with about a hundred vehicles, the procession to Kandahar crossed the border from Pakistan into Afghanistan. Karzai felt bound by his honor to return his father's body to his hometown. The funeral procession traveled without weapons through the heart of Taliban country in southern Afghanistan. It was here that the Taliban had its greatest support.

Karzai's gamble paid off. The Taliban could have easily attacked his convoy. It even positioned tanks in and around Kandahar before Karzai arrived. In the end, it did nothing. Karzai had come as a civilian and as a son. Perhaps the Taliban feared dishonoring such a traditional Afghan tradition. Karzai thought the Taliban was frightened because many Afghans were becoming tired of its rule. For Karzai, it was a sign that the Taliban was vulnerable.

CHAPTER THREE

A PATRIOT RETURNS

Karzai had warned the international community about Osama bin Laden early on. Karzai told the Academy of Achievement, "I told the French, I told the U.S., I told the Europeans that this somebody called Osama [and the Taliban] are bringing in horrible people from the Arab world, from Pakistan, and these are killers." Karzai was rarely home at the end of the 1990s. He was traveling around the world trying to get help for Afghanistan.

In 2000, Karzai appeared before the U.S. Senate Foreign Relations Committee. He warned its members that if they did not address the problem of the Taliban soon, then the United States, and possibly the world, was in great danger.

OSAMA BIN LADEN AND 9/11

Soon after moving to Afghanistan, Osama bin Laden began creating training camps to train

Osama bin Laden, pictured here at an undisclosed location in Afghanistan, is still the most wanted man in the world, years after the September 11 terror attacks.

new mujahideen to attack Western influences in the Muslim world. By the late 1990s, he was often seen with Mullah Omar and other high-ranking Taliban leaders. From Afghanistan, he trained Al Qaeda terrorists, who later went on to attack targets in the Muslim world and also in the West.

It was the September 11, 2001, attacks on the United States that finally made bin Laden America's public enemy number one. After more than three thousand people were killed by nineteen airline hijackers, the United States decided to invade Afghanistan. American forces aimed to overthrow the Taliban regime, destroy the training camps, and punish those mujahideen allied with bin Laden.

KARZAI TAKES ACTION

After 9/11, Karzai went to the U.S. embassy in Islamabad, Pakistan, to talk with U.S. officials about bin Laden and the Taliban. He had been warning the world for years; now that the worst terrorist attack of the modern era had occurred, he offered his help. U.S. officials were skeptical: would the Afghan people help overthrow the Taliban?

Karzai was positive that they would, having long felt oppressed under the Taliban. He also knew that the United States would be moving soon to punish those who had attacked it, and that the Afghan people had a poor chance at freedom unless the United States helped them.

Karzai asked some of his colleagues whether they thought the United States would help them overthrow Afghanistan's rulers. They doubted it. Karzai insisted it would, telling them, "Think of New York. Think of what happened there. The world has woken up. Let's move into Afghanistan. Let's move into the heart of the Taliban." Once again, Karzai was willing to risk life and limb on a mission into the middle of enemy territory.

ON DANGEROUS GROUND

Before he departed for Afghanistan, Karzai warned the colleagues that would go with him that they had a 60 percent chance of death and a 40 percent chance of survival. They could barely imagine at that point that they could win over the Taliban. The next morning, with three colleagues on two motorcycles, and a single

A June 19, 2001, frame of an Al Qaeda–produced tape shows members of the terrorist organization performing drills with AK-47 Kalashnikov rifles at the Al-Farouq training camp.

satellite phone between the four of them, they crossed the border into Afghanistan.

Problems almost derailed the whole mission from the start. Four flat tires made Karzai nearly panic. They snuck into Kandahar, the center of Taliban power in the south, and hid at a nearby villager's house. In the morning, the villager expressed his concern that Karzai could not possibly achieve his goal with so few followers. Karzai answered that everyone hated the Taliban, and that he had been working on the problem for years. The fire just needed a spark.

The helpful villager told them that they would surely be captured if they stayed near the city. So the villager arranged to have them taken to the safety of the central mountains of Afghanistan. There, they could use the natural terrain to hide, or at least to fight from a position of advantage.

Karzai and the others used disguises—local clothing, for example—so as not to arouse suspicion. Driving for a long time, they reached the province of Uruzgan, where they spent the night.

WARTIME DIPLOMAT

The next day, Karzai contacted a friend—a local mullah (religious leader)—in a nearby village, asking him to have dinner that night. The message came back to Karzai that he should only travel by night, and on foot. The friend would send a guide to lead Karzai and his team along the way.

The way was long and hard. The guide took them in many directions, sometimes over the same ground. They had to make sure no one was tracking them and also avoid seeing other people. When they reached Karzai's friend, he was surprised they had made it to him alive. He was even more shocked that Karzai was trying to start a rebellion against the Taliban.

After dinner, the mullah wanted to know how they aimed to beat their enemies. He thought that Karzai should ask the United States for military air support. Karzai disagreed: He didn't want to expose innocent Afghans to devastating air attacks. The friend also told Karzai that unless he asked for U.S. air support, then he obviously was not serious about really overthrowing the Taliban. He told Karzai, as quoted by the Academy of Achievement, "I'm not going to allow you to kill my children and woman because of your desire to defeat the Taliban with the two or three guns we have."

Karzai realized that his friend was willing to risk his own life and the lives of his family and friends for freedom, but only if Karzai was willing to be realistic. They would need all the help they could get. He soon traveled to another village to gain more support.

THE REBELLION GROWS

Word soon came that about 1,500 Taliban and Al Qaeda fighters were heading their way. Karzai says that this was the first time he heard the term "Al Qaeda," which means "the base" in Arabic. The foreign Arabs, Pakistanis, and native Afghans who had trained in bin Laden's terrorist camps had taken it as an informal name. Once again, Karzai aimed for the mountains. This time, more volunteers joined his group, raising the total to fifty.

On their way through the mountains, Karzai was amazed that the traditional Afghan sense of hospitality remained, even under terrible conditions. A poor family of four fed fifty men the first day. Word had begun to spread about Karzai and his men. On the second day, forty more showed up. By the third, their ranks had swelled to 120. Still, the villagers fed them. It was an inspiring moment for the rebels. Despite the odds against them, the pride that Karzai felt for his countrymen kept him going.

A PLEA FOR HELP

Support was trickling in, but Karzai knew that time was running out. They still would be out-numbered, and they had few weapons and no money to buy more. A group of villagers from nearby came to Karzai offering their support. Karzai quickly decided to contact the Americans for help.

Karzai finally got through to the U.S. embassy in Islamabad. Embassy officials, too, were amazed he was still alive. Word of his mission had reached them somehow. To his surprise, they agreed to send weapons. Karzai gave the Americans a general idea of his location. In turn, they told him to prepare four fires in a square pattern, 100 meters (328 feet) on each side. That way, they would identify exactly where he was.

THE FIRST SKIRMISH

Within the next couple of days, Karzai and his supporters had obtained fifteen parcels of weapons, ammunition, and food from three American planes. They had to scramble to get some of it, but they grabbed the last of the supplies just in time. A villager woke Karzai up at 4:30 in the morning the day after the final supplies arrived with the news that about four hundred Taliban troops were approaching.

Soon, their enemies found Karzai and his troops. With bullets flying, they were still outnumbered and outgunned, with no means of communication. Karzai retreated to a mountaintop. To save their small force, Karzai's men decided to split into many small groups and escape. Fortunately, the Taliban had decided to retreat. News of the Northern Alliance attacks from the north had scared the defenders of the south.

From then on, they won battle after battle without firing a single shot. Taliban fighters in each town surrendered, ran away, or switched to Karzai's side. Karzai felt vindicated: his belief that most Afghans were ready to get rid of their harsh rulers was true. Everywhere they went, only the most dedicated Taliban forces ran off to fight another day. The rest welcomed Karzai with open arms.

THE INVASION

Many miles away, equally important events were taking place. The United States invaded Afghanistan in October 2001. The start of the campaign was a huge air assault directed at the Taliban. The bombing started on October 7, 2001. On the ground, American Special Forces mobilized to aid the soldiers of the Northern Alliance. CIA special agents also aided in many cases.

For the last few years, the Northern Alliance had controlled only 5 percent of Afghanistan. With American air support and U.S. Special Forces and CIA operatives—and former Taliban allies switching to their side—this would soon change quickly.

Northern Alliance troops in the foreground march on November 18, 2001, as U.S. planes bomb distant targets near the Taliban-controlled city of Kunduz, Afghanistan.

Special Forces are the best of the American military, the most experienced soldiers who go into unfriendly areas with little support from larger groups of soldiers. These Special Forces were deployed throughout Afghanistan, and Karzai would soon meet some of them.

KARZAI GETS A SPECIAL BOOST

Well into Karzai's now not-so-secret campaign against the Taliban, U.S. Special Forces were sent to help him. Among the first were the men of Operational Detachment Alpha (ODA) 574, an eleven-man team. They knew little about Karzai at first, but they soon learned that he was the man behind a rebellion against the Taliban. Behind the scenes, Karzai was being considered as a possible leader of a postwar Afghanistan.

On the ground, the Special Forces wanted to unite with him because he was an influential figure. He had already motivated a large group of anti-Taliban tribesmen to fight. Also, he was a Pashtun and would serve as the vital link between American and Afghan efforts in the war.

A RELUCTANT COMMANDER?

U.S. Army captain Jason Amerine led ODA 574. He revealed to the PBS news show *Frontline*: "When we first were told that we were linking up with Hamid Karzai, that name had no meaning to us. We were pretty quickly given information about who he was. So we were able to figure out that this was a pretty important figure." Despite his status as a Pashtun resistance leader, Karzai shied away from being a military leader. He simply felt that he was the spark that would ignite the rebellion. Captain Amerine had to balance this need of Karzai's with his own need to organize a fighting force in the south that would be able to meet the better-equipped and more numerous Taliban forces.

THE BATTLE OF TARIN KOWT

Karzai decided with the Special Forces commanders that the next logical step was to take the town of Tarin Kowt. According to Captain Amerine, Karzai saw it as "the heart of the Taliban movement." All the major leaders of the Taliban, including Mullah Omar, had family and allies there. Winning Tarin Kowt was, therefore, a huge psychological victory.

Also, only a handful of the Taliban forces were very dedicated. Many simply fought with the Taliban because they feared it. Once they saw that Karzai and the Americans were victorious, they would switch sides. Karzai explained that most undecided Afghans would go with the winning team. If anti-Taliban forces took the town, they would win thousands of new converts. The rest would surrender or run away.

Karzai told Captain Amerine that he had some supporters in Tarin Kowt. While there were hundreds of volunteers, many of them had to stay put and defend their own villages against Taliban attacks. In the end, they had, at most, sixty men available to take and hold the town. Another big surprise was yet to come.

On November 16, 2001, the town of Tarin Kowt rebelled, driving out the Taliban adminis-trators. Immediately, Karzai insisted that they go and take over the town while the opportunity was there. Amerine was wary: they didn't have enough men to defend the town if the Taliban waged a counterattack. But Amerine decided that Karzai was right. After a whole day of travel, ready for a bloody firefight, they arrive to find a quiet, subdued scene at Tarin Kowt.

Karzai immediately arranged to meet with local Pashtun leaders, while Amerine prepared for the defense of the town. News of a Taliban force of about 500 men in about 100 vehicles reached him. With a force only one-fifth the size of their enemies, Amerine had to plan out his strategy carefully.

Karzai had eyes and ears everywhere through his Pashtun allies in the region. His biggest tool was the satellite phone. He contacted friendly Pashtuns throughout the province and beyond to find out what the Taliban was up to next.

Amerine also admired Karzai's diplomatic strategy when dealing with the local tribal leaders. Quite intentionally, Karzai never picked a second-in-command, even though that meant he had to do almost everything by himself. Amerine told Frontline, "If he'd picked [one particular] tribal leader, [telling him] 'You're my second in command,' then his cousins and brothers and so on would have all suddenly become a favored group of tribes, which would have made these other tribes angry. So he really couldn't afford to designate a second in command."

THE BEGINNING OF THE END FOR THE TALIBAN

With good air support, and a command of the high ground at Tarin Kowt, Amerine's defensive force of around forty men was able to defeat a group of Taliban fighters many times larger. Karzai stepped in and assured the local mullahs and other Afghans that this was the beginning of the end for their enemies.

The anti-Taliban forces had won a great victory. If it had gone the other way, Karzai would

Shown here in December 2001 is an Afghan in a cave in Tora Bora, Afghanistan, a former hiding place for Al Qaeda and Taliban troops.

have lost all credibility with the rest of the Afghans in the region. Karzai, Amerine, and the forces they had gathered soon moved on to attack Taliban and Al Qaeda forces near Kandahar. Before Kandahar could be taken, the Northern Alliance took the capital, Kabul, on November 13, 2001.

Kandahar was a holdout, but the city fell to Karzai and his U.S. allies in the first week of December. The initial ground war was over, and the Taliban was on the run. Osama bin Laden and Mullah Omar had escaped despite some close calls, but the ultimate goal of Karzai had been realized: a newly freed Afghanistan.

CHAPTER FOUR

KARZAI RISING

Restoring a country that had been at war for the previous two decades was not an overnight process. At the end of 2001, Afghanistan was among the poorest countries in the world. Much of its infrastructure—buildings, roads, etc.—had been destroyed. Old rivalries among members of the Northern Alliance threatened to flare up. Much like the end of the Soviet occupation, the power vacuum left by the defeat of the Taliban made the country's future uncertain.

THE BONN AGREEMENT

One big step for Afghanistan was a conference held in Bonn, Germany, on December 5, 2001, while Karzai was still helping finish off the Taliban near Kandahar. Exiled Afghan political leaders met at Bonn to decide on an interim (temporary) leader of the nation, as well as a twenty-nine-member governing committee.

After much negotiation, Karzai was informed by telephone that he was, for now, the leader of Afghanistan. He admitted that he could not fully concentrate on the news because many of his fellow rebels had just suffered a bomb attack and he was busy tending to the wounded.

He was confirmed in a ceremony on December 22. Though some criticized the conference—most of the leaders had no real support among common Afghans—Karzai was a unifying figure who had good relations with Pashtuns and the ethnic minorities who made up much of the Northern Alliance. The conference also set certain goals for a new government to achieve, such as a constitution and other aims.

Soon thereafter, Karzai once again appealed to the international community, this time for money instead of military support. At an international

Newly appointed Afghan interim president Hamid Karzai takes the presidential oath in Kabul on December 22, 2001, not long after he helped overthrow the Taliban.

donors conference in Tokyo, Japan, in January 2002, he won pledges of up to $4 billion to help rebuild his war-ravaged nation. It would prove to be a small drop in the bucket for a country that basically had to rebuild from the ground up.

KARZAI AS A STATESMAN

Karzai's political skills would be tested from now on like never before. The Taliban was on the run, but in its place were a group of warlords, each with his own territory and his own idea to govern the people under his rule. Karzai knew many of them, had even worked with them via phone during the overthrow of the Taliban.

Karzai needed the support of the warlords to rebuild. In June 2002, a longtime dream of Karzai's was realized: a Loya Jirga was convened. This grand council, an ancient Afghan tradition, brought together tribal chiefs, warlords, and other important leaders to decide on important issues. The June meeting reappointed Karzai as the head of state, among other things.

DEVASTATION, BUT HOPE

Karzai and other Afghans were now left to pick up the pieces of a war-torn nation. All the problems of a third-world nation, plus reconstructing after the war and preventing the return of the Taliban and Al Qaeda, made this a tall order. In 2002, the average life expectancy for an Afghan was forty-three years of age. Afghanistan ranked as the world's fifth poorest nation.

Initially, Karzai and others were optimistic. With the Taliban gone, people had started enjoying some of the freedoms and privileges that Americans take for granted. Karzai told the Academy of Achievement conference in Dublin, Ireland, in June 2002, that one of his greatest pleasures in life was seeing the rise of schools. He said, "It's the best sight for me. I spend the whole day very happy . . . when I see the Afghan children going to school." The *New York Times* wrote in October 2006 that between five and six million children in Afghanistan now attend school, two million of which are girls.

Karzai's efforts on the international front also seemed promising. The United States alone provided $909 million in 2002 to Afghanistan for rebuilding efforts. U.S. aid increased from $962 million in 2004 to $1.5 billion in 2005.

Non-governmental organizations (NGOs) seemed to flood Afghanistan in the year after the war. Among them were women's groups, foreign health-care organizations, and other aid groups. Many were eager to rebuild and help retrieve the country from its hard-line Islamic militant past. The Afghan government and others set about restoring the country's almost useless roads and highways.

THE CONSTITUTIONAL LOYA JIRGA

After the initial major Loya Jirga that reappointed Karzai as interim leader in June 2002, one of Karzai's biggest victories was the December 2003 constitutional Loya Jirga. Five hundred and two delegates representing Afghanistan's numerous ethnic groups came together to decide

Safia Siddiqi *(right)*, a vice chairperson of Afghanistan's Loya Jirga, talks while seated with fellow vice chairpersons Mirwais Yasini and Mohammad Azam Dadfar during a December 2003 press conference.

on important issues. After intense bargaining, the results, made official on January 4, 2004, left Karzai optimistic. Women were now considered, at least on paper, to have rights equal to that of men.

Another result was the extension of full rights to ethnic minorities. This included the right to maintain their local traditions, including schooling in their respective languages. For groups such as the Uzbeks and Tajiks, it was a huge relief; many had believed that Karzai, a Pashtun, would favor his own ethnic group. For years, Pashtuns had dominated the government and passed laws in their own favor. As Afghanistan's largest ethnic group, with 40 percent of the population, they had sometimes overrode the wishes of the other groups.

A system of civil law was also established that satisfied most parties. The laws were generally more progressive than many other Islamic societies. However, no law was allowed that the majority viewed to be contrary to the Islamic faith.

A STARK REALITY

Despite these grand developments, the legacy of violence and oppression of the last two decades had deep roots. Many Taliban fighters found refuge in neighboring Pakistan. Others blended into their local villages easily; clan and tribe affiliations—and sometimes intimidation— often undercut support for a president in remote Kabul. Bin Laden and Mullah Omar were still on the run, and untold numbers of Al Qaeda operatives had escaped.

In addition, the war had destroyed a good deal of usable roads and buildings in Afghanistan. Some aid organizations were shocked at just how deprived Afghanistan was. In remote areas, far from cities such as Kabul, conditions were even worse. The *New York Times* reported in 2004 that many groups arriving in late 2001 had to build their own headquarters due to lack of usable buildings. Karzai admitted that a lack of resources was a big problem for his country.

RAISING AN ARMY

Afghanistan faced problems with its human resources as well. Karzai has often complained that progress in Afghanistan has been delayed by the competing interests of the warlords. A local farmer in the area of Lashkar Gah, a town once held up as an example of Afghanistan's successes, lamented the situation. He told the *New York Times*, "We don't have law. This is a warlord kingdom."

One of the problems is the simple lack of military forces. The United States began training a new Afghan National Army (ANA) in 2002. The aim was to create a unified military that would one day replace the 100,000 or so estimated soldiers who belong to individual warlords. Without it, Karzai concedes, Afghanistan will never be a real nation.

Problems with ANA arose almost immediately. In 2002, Robert Finn, the American ambassador to Afghanistan, did a review of the newest recruits and found them sorely lacking. The troops lacked discipline—in some cases, even basic skills. "They were illiterate," he told the *New York Times*. "They didn't know how to keep themselves clean. They were at a much lower level than people expected."

The police were even more challenging. Seventy percent of the 80,000 police officers at the time could not read. Many of them did not do their jobs, but simply took bribes for tasks they should have been doing anyway, such as responding to reports of crimes.

To date, the United States is still not fully confident in the ability of the ANA to take over security in Afghanistan any time soon. As of early 2006, the ANA had merely 35,000 troops, well shy of the 70,000 the United States hoped to train before allowing Afghanistan complete control over its own security.

While Hamid Karzai speaks several languages, he is an exception in Afghanistan. Many troops come from different backgrounds and do not speak, read, or write the same language. Trainers have had to improvise, using visual aids for soldiers who either do not understand the training given in the national language, Dari, or who are simply illiterate. For years, the only skills necessary for young men were farming or fighting, especially under the Taliban, who disdained most education, except for religious instruction.

PRESIDENT KARZAI—
A HISTORIC MOMENT

Despite the drawbacks, Karzai has helped usher his nation into a new, historical era: that of democracy. The year 2004 marked a tough year of transition for Afghanistan: slower-than-expected reconstruction and military training and a resurgence of the Taliban and other antigovernment violence, among other problems. But the leadup to the October 9 presidential elections was nonetheless exciting for many Afghans, including their interim president.

Karzai had several factors in his favor as he stood for election for president. He was well-known among the populace, having led the country for more than two and a half years.

While there had been an upsurge of violence against American troops that year, a great many Afghans were still pro-American. They were grateful to the United States, and its president, George W. Bush, for helping to push out the Taliban. Karzai took full advantage of Bush's endorsement. Shrewdly, he even drove in a U.S. Army transport vehicle during the campaign.

Another element was the short campaign season. Unlike in the United States, where political coverage of an election can start as early as two years before, Afghanistan's presidential race was only a month long. Some Afghans and other observers criticized this. They claimed that Karzai was so well-known that the short campaign season could not help but benefit him.

Most of the other choices for president were unfamiliar to the common Afghan citizen. Slate.com reported that some candidates, and even voters, were frustrated by this. A voter in Jalalabad complained, "Tell me about someone beside Karzai, and I will vote for them. But who is there?"

Some of them even had harsh words for Karzai's relationship with the United States. One candidate, a poet named Latif Pedram, told Slate.com, "Karzai is a mindless leader—he does whatever the foreigners tell him." This is a common complaint of the president's critics.

Right before the election, there were fears of Taliban interference and attacks on voting stations. But election day came and went relatively quietly. The United Nations actually investigated voter fraud that may have favored the incumbent president. It found no concrete evidence of any tampering.

About 4.3 million of 8.1 million votes cast (55.4 percent) went to Karzai. He won twenty-one of the thirty-four Afghan provinces. He was now the official, democratically elected president, the first in Afghanistan's modern history. A century of monarchical, Communist, and Islamist extremist rule had come to an end.

On December 7, 2004, Hamid Karzai was sworn in as president of Afghanistan during a formal ceremony in Kabul. For Karzai and his supporters, and for the United States, too, this

On October 9, 2004, Afghan women are pictured with their voting cards during election day in the southern city of Kandahar, marking the first direct presidential election in Afghanistan's history.

represented a new beginning for the war-ravaged nation. The last three surviving presidents of the country also attended, as did King Zahir Shah.

Karzai thanked the United States: "Today whatever we have achieved—the peace . . . the reconstruction . . . the fact that Afghanistan is again a respected member of the international community—because of the help that the United States of America gave us."

ANOTHER ROUND OF DEMOCRACY

In 2005, Afghanistan was again getting ready for new elections, this time to select members of the Afghan Parliament. Karzai was busy working behind the scenes and in public, too. Keeping the 2005 election trouble-free was especially important to Karzai. He had to prove that the country's first experience with democracy in 2004 was the first of many. The field of candidates for office was enormous: over 5,000 filed to become members of the National Assembly and the provincial assemblies.

Before the elections, Karzai visited the United States in May. He was grateful for a very warm welcome from the American public during his trip. The Center for Afghan Studies at the University of Nebraska at Omaha awarded him an honorary degree. Later, Boston University in Boston, Massachusetts, also awarded him a degree.

At a press conference with President Bush at the White House, Karzai gave thanks to the

U.S. president George W. Bush and Afghan president Hamid Karzai shake hands at an Oval Office meeting at the White House on May 23, 2005.

United States for helping Afghanistan through tough times. "Neither our press, nor yours, nor the press in the rest of the world will pick up the miseries of the Afghans three years ago, and what has been achieved since then, until today. We have a Constitution; we had a presidential election—and I'm glad it turned out to be good for me," Karzai joked.

CHAPTER FIVE

KARZAI AND AFGHANISTAN

It has been a long road for Hamid Karzai. He has seen his country go from kingdom to war zone to unsteady democracy. More than five years after the U.S. invasion, Afghanistan remains at a crossroads.

MILESTONES

Karzai gave a measure of Afghanistan's progress at a meeting in Kabul with U.S. secretary of state Condoleezza Rice on June 28, 2006. He said, "There is absolute certainty that Afghanistan is going to strengthen the gains of the past five years. Whatever was asked of the Afghan people in the Bonn agreement has been fulfilled on time. We have a constitution, elections for the president, a very vibrant parliament and a strengthening civil society." He went on to list other improvements: the building of schools, new road construction, improving farms, and the return of 4.5 million Afghan refugees back home.

A reporter from Bloomberg News, however, asked Karzai whether he had concerns about the return of the Taliban. Specifically, she wondered whether Karzai could travel freely in the south of Afghanistan, where Pashtun support for the Taliban was strongest. Karzai responded that the media sometimes only concentrated on the negative. He insisted there were many good things happening in Afghanistan, but that sometimes these weren't reported properly. However, economic problems, the continuing threat of the Taliban, and the warlords who maintain a sometimes uneasy partnership with Karzai are influential in shaping the Afghanistan of today.

"NOTHING FOR US"

Zoraiya, a nineteen-year-old Afghan who was once a refugee in Pakistan, speaking with *Time* magazine in July 2006 expressed an all-too-common complaint about life now in Afghanistan. "When Karzai became president he told us there would be homes and jobs, but there is nothing for us," said Zoraiya. "If he

A farmer leads his cows through a poppy field in the northeastern Afghan region of Badakhshan on May 29, 2005. Afghanistan remains the world's largest source for heroin and opium.

gave us the [bus] fare, we'd move back to Pakistan." Others also complain that Kabul has seen a great deal of foreign money, but that in the heartland of Afghanistan, where most of the people live, there is still great poverty. Many people have no electricity or running water, much less jobs.

APPEASING THE WARLORDS

For many years, power in Afghanistan has been held by the warlords who rule its various provinces. Critics have said that Karzai has been far too easy on them. Recently, *Time* reported that many Afghans were angry that several high-ranking warlords were given important jobs in the nation's police force. For Karzai, this may have been a way of keeping his "enemies" where he could see them.

In uprooting the Taliban, both Karzai and American officials recognized the value of the warlords, as many Afghans viewed membership in a tribe or a warlord's personal military force as being more important than broader national issues. As military analyst Joanna Nathan told *Time*, "They wanted a war on the cheap. They co-opted old mujahideen warlords and militia leaders to fight the Taliban." To some, this was a devil's bargain because now the warlords have great power not only in their own regions, but in Karzai's government. It is harder than ever before to control them.

A HOUSE DIVIDED

Deadly squabbles between rival warlords have plagued Afghanistan for many years. Karzai's Afghan National Army (ANA) is often ineffectual in stopping the violence. Often, the United States and NATO must step in to calm things down.

Veteran commander Ismail Khan, now Afghanistan's minister of energy, was attacked in August 2004 by Amanullah Khan, a rival. As many as twenty fighters were killed during the fight, with the ANA having to broker a cease-fire. Some observers think that it was only the presence of American airpower right after the fighting that made the combatants stop the battle.

Other warlords have turned sides against Karzai and his Western allies. Gulbuddin Hekmatyr, another mujahideen leader of some influence in the Northern Alliance, declared jihad against foreign troops in 2002. Many think that he has allied himself with his former enemies, the Taliban. In November 2003, the U.S. Army's 10th Mountain Division led an unsuccessful mission to find Hekmatyr and his followers.

Ismail Khan, pictured here on February 11, 2002, answering a question at a press conference in Herat, western Afghanistan, remains one of the most powerful warlords with whom Karzai must deal.

Other supposedly "friendly" warlords are also suspected Taliban collaborators. U.S. military forces have complained that they have been misled by the warlords about Taliban activity. Once again, not everything in Afghanistan is as it seems, and Karzai and his friends must take every bit of information with a grain of salt.

Many people are angry that Ismail Khan is even a minister in Karzai's government. On one hand, he is considered to be one of the most corrupt and oppressive of the warlords, especially when it comes to punishing perceived anti-Islamic behavior such as drinking and indecency. But others consider Karzai a pragmatist who knows the value of keeping potential enemies (like Khan) on the side of the central government. Otherwise, Karzai risks making enemies among his most powerful allies.

KARZAI AND HUMAN RIGHTS

With the Afghan National Army still relatively weak, the warlords have made their own rules in their own regions. Ismail Khan, for example, has been harshly criticized by human rights groups for his province's treatment of women. Khan was once governor of Herat, and his firing from that post provoked two days of riots. Even after he eventually decided to step down, he remains the most powerful figure in Herat.

After the fall of the Taliban, images filled the news in the United States of women liberated from burkas, off to school, and finally free. It was one of the most important public relations victories for the U.S.-led effort. But the situation is more complicated than that. In Herat, Khan earned harsh criticism from Human Rights Watch (HRW), a well-known NGO that tracks and tries to stop human rights abuses world-wide. HRW reported in December 2002 that Khan had reformed the Taliban-era Ministry of Vice and Virtue. This was a police force that strictly enforced modesty. They made sure that women were not seen with male nonrelatives and did not drive cars, and even performed impromptu chastity tests to see if a woman had had sex recently. They enforced strict dress codes and even beat men and women who were considered lawbreakers.

A WOMAN'S PLACE?

At his June 2006 press conference with President George W. Bush at the White House in Washington, D.C., Karzai touched on the issue of women's rights in his country. "There are women from all the provinces of the country [that] will be coming to the Parliament. So the country is moving forward," said Karzai. President Bush also noted then that "a shift of opinion is taking place where now women are equal partners in society; over 40 percent of

Afghan girls read during class on October 8, 2006, near Puli Alam, Logar province. Taliban rebels have been threatening to attack or forcibly close girls' schools in the region.

the voters on that October day were women voters; girls are now going to school; women entrepreneurs are opening businesses."

Despite Karzai and Bush's claims of progress, all is not well when it comes to women's rights in Afghanistan. Ismail Khan's city of Herat is not an isolated case. In the city of Lashkar Gah, for example, the United States built a job-training center for women in 2004. Lashkar Gah was a unique city in Afghanistan to begin with: the amount of construction and development by the United States led many to call the city "Little America." Fowzea Olomi, a local activist for women's rights, ran the center.

But the growing power of the Taliban in Lashkar Gah made life dangerous for U.S.-supported activists. In May, not long before Karzai's visit to the White House, Olomi's driver was shot dead. Olomi told the *New York Times* at the time that she was afraid they would target her next. "Our government is weak," she said. "Anarchy has come."

The Revolutionary Association of the Women of Afghanistan (RAWA) also agreed with this assessment. RAWA, founded in Kabul by student activist Meena Keshwar Kamal in 1977 (later assassinated for her political beliefs), is a controversial group. With members in Afghanistan and Pakistan, it has often angered some Afghans. This is because it opposes all forms of religious fundamentalism. RAWA harshly criticized Karzai. It said that he has no power outside of Kabul, and that he therefore is doing little, if anything, to help the plight of women stuck in places like Herat.

THE TALIBAN RETURNS

In recent years, the Taliban has bounced back from its defeat in 2001. Osama bin Laden and Mullah Omar, among other high-ranking leaders, remain at large. Many former Taliban mujahideen escaped to Pakistan or elsewhere. The Pakistani areas closest to the border with Afghanistan remain a hotbed of Taliban support despite U.S. and Pakistani efforts to arrest or kill insurgents there.

Other Taliban fighters have blended in throughout Afghanistan. In the south, many areas are in fact controlled by the Taliban, especially Pashtun areas. Karzai's military, even with American and NATO help, is still struggling to defeat it.

A 2006 report by the CIA outlined this struggle, the *New York Times* reported in November of that year. One of the greatest

A foot patrol of the Panjwayi district in the province of Kandahar on November 8, 2006, is comprised of Afghan National Army troops and Canadians from the Royal 22nd Regiment.

problems is "the ability [of Karzai's government] to project into the countryside," the report stated.

ESCALATION

For a time, suicide attacks and roadside bombs were relatively unknown in Afghanistan. Over the last few years, however, they have escalated. Many Afghans now feel less safe than they have in years. Taliban insurgents have targeted U.S. forces,

NGOs, women's groups, journalists, and especially Afghans who support Karzai and his American and European allies.

The motivations of the attacks remain complex, an unnamed senior American official in Afghanistan told the New York Times. "How much of this is support for the Taliban?" he asked. "How much is coerced? How much of it is gun for hire? How much of it is a young man who has nothing else to do and this sounds pretty exciting? Our analysis is that there's some degree of all of those." Other American officials agreed that popular support for the Taliban is no longer confined to the Pakistani border areas. In Afghanistan, it is gaining more supporters.

As of November 2006, at least 143 American and NATO soldiers had been killed by Taliban fighters that year, 55 more than in 2005. The United States initially planned to withdraw as many as 3,000 troops from Afghanistan, but the latest fighting prompted it to cancel the withdrawal. Ronald E. Neumann, a U.S. ambassador to Kabul, said that America faced "stark choices" in the country. He told the *New York Times*, "We're going to have to stay at it. Or we're going to fail and the country will fall apart again."

At the end of October 2006, NATO and Afghan forces killed as many as seventy Taliban fighters in a night battle in the province of Uruzgan—the same place where Karzai began his revolt against the Taliban five years earlier. The battle was part of a much larger NATO offensive against a rising Taliban.

Civilian casualties have also risen greatly in recent months. In response, President Karzai called for better teamwork between Afghan and NATO forces to prevent civilian deaths. This was in the wake of the deaths of dozens of noncombatants during NATO air strikes against Taliban targets in Kandahar.

Even schools are not safe. In 2005, 146 schools in Afghanistan were attacked. In the first ten months of 2006, the number rose to 160, the *New York Times* reported. Most of these have been the result of nighttime arson attacks. Ten schools in Helmand province were closed for ten months until October 2006.

Hamid Karzai walks with President George W. Bush and Pakistani president Pervez Musharraf after a speech in the White House Rose Garden on September 27, 2006.

AFGHANISTAN AND PAKISTAN AT ODDS

There are many factors that are frustrating Karzai's efforts: popular support for the Taliban in many areas; the sense that his government is corrupt and not working well; his lack of military might outside of Kabul; and the inability of Pakistan to deal with its own Islamic extremists.

Karzai has been at odds with Pakistani president Pervez Musharraf, demanding that Musharraf do more to defeat Taliban support in Pakistan. But Musharraf, though holding greater power in his own country than Karzai does in Afghanistan, has had a hard time doing so. The ISI, his intelligence service, and many Islamic fundamentalists in his country are actively supporting the Taliban's return in Afghanistan. During an appearance on PBS's *Frontline*, Karzai said, "We have exact information that in the madrassas [hard-line religious schools] of Pakistan, young boys are being told to go to Afghanistan and join the jihad."

Musharraf responded angrily to Karzai's statements, saying, "Who is doing anything? Is Karzai doing something? Are they doing anything? Their whole countryside is rampant with Taliban today. When they are not being able to control that, they shift blame to Pakistan."

The Taliban continues to use the Pakistani border areas to launch attacks across the border. Again, the complicated issue of tribal loyalty comes up: Steve Coll, Pulitzer Prize–winning author of a book on military intelligence, *Ghost Wars*, said of the Pashtun tribesmen that populate those areas: "When the Pakistan army is fighting the Taliban, they're fighting cousins. They're fighting brethren."

KARZAI: DEFIANT, BUT CAUTIOUS

On November 1, 2006, Karzai made a rare trip out of his palace, reported Reuters. Most likely, he wanted to refute accusations that he is out of touch and in constant danger of his life being taken. The article stated that, aside from trips abroad and around Afghanistan, it was only the third time he had physically walked in the streets of Kabul. He accepted a free loaf from a local Afghan restaurant. It was a symbolic gesture: the same block was the target of a devastating suicide attack in September 2006. Like the funeral procession to take his father home, it was a typical Karzai moment. The president of Afghanistan is a cautious diplomat who must show his strength to a nation desperately seeking peace and prosperity.

CHAPTER SIX

WHAT'S NEXT?

Fred Kaplan wrote in the *Nation* in June 2006 about NATO's gigantic headquarters in Kandahar, ground zero for the Taliban resistance in the south of the nation. It was, ironically, also the center for British troop actions in the nineteenth century, when Great Britain tried to control Afghanistan. The Soviet Union also had a base there before it was forced to abandon the war it waged against the mujahideen in the 1980s. One British officer told Kaplan that the base is "one of the busiest military airfields in the world."

Kaplan wrote that "the Western campaign here is huge, much bigger than most press accounts indicate." Even with a large Western troop presence, terrible attacks occur all the time. In early 2006, insurgents blew up a bus transporting local workers being taken to help build up the airfield at the base. Kaplan observed during his visit to Afghanistan that NATO looks ready to stay in Afghanistan for the long haul.

For Karzai and Afghanistan, the future is in the balance. In September 2006, Karzai appeared before the United Nations General Assembly in New York. He called his nation the "worst victim" of terrorism. He pleaded with the international community to help Afghanistan root out the Taliban and its allies not only in Afghanistan, but around the world. He said, "You have to look beyond Afghanistan to the sources of terrorism." His country's greatest challenge—fighting the Taliban—was robbing children of education, curtailing efforts to improve the economy and health care, and taking innocent lives, both from Taliban attacks and accidental killings by the United States and NATO.

Karzai will finish his term in 2008, and he does not plan, at this time, to run for president again. Observers note that it must indeed be a hard life, and exhausting. He has worked endless days for the last few years. News reports seldom mention that Karzai spends very little time with his family; he married his wife Zinat, an obstetrician, in 1998. They have no children. Karzai's brother, Ahmed Wali Karzai,

United States First Lady Laura Bush meets with Zinat Karzai, the wife of Hamid Karzai, at the Presidential Palace in Kabul, Afghanistan, in March 2006.

is a coordinator for humanitarian assistance in their hometown province of Kandahar. His other siblings own restaurants in the U.S. cities of San Francisco, California; Baltimore, Maryland; and Cambridge, Massachusetts. Karzai once said that his eventual retirement will, if nothing else, allow him to see his family more.

But for Karzai, it has been a road well worth the ride. He reminds his detractors that

Afghanistan has come a long way, despite the recent problems. He admits that attacks are on the rise and that his nation faces serious problems, but that these are challenges that he will face with them. He has become more vocal in recent months about the need for more international support—he is only one man, and he cannot change everything single-handedly.

For many, from the allies critical of him to the Taliban, Karzai is a puppet of the Western powers, installed in the presidency to keep Afghanistan stable. For his enemies, Karzai has given up power to the warlords and is powerless to stop the rise of the Taliban.

Karzai's supporters counter that he is a natural diplomat who has simply taken the traditional Afghan way of governing—cooperation,

Karzai plays the traditional Afghan sport of jousting on May 29, 2003, while on a trip to meet with Afghan people in Ghazni, southwest of Kabul.

consensus, alliances—to a new level. In the process, he has brought Afghanistan out of the Taliban era. Afghanistan now has a constitution and a Parliament that represents women more equally than most other Muslim nations, and is struggling to free itself of the old ways of extremism. Karzai's dream of seeing Afghan children returning to school has come true. Despite the struggle, for this Afghan freedom fighter, patriot, statesman, and leader, it has been well worth it.

THE NEXT CHALLENGE

For Karzai, in the present time, the next couple of years are the true proving ground for whether Afghanistan joins the community of nations or returns to radical Islam. The players that will decide this great game include Karzai himself, the international community, the warlords he must depend on (but must control as well), and the Taliban and Al Qaeda. The story is still unfolding, and a resurgence of anti-Karzai forces is perhaps the greatest threat to stability.

As Karzai told the Academy of Achievement in Dublin, Ireland, "We have a duty before our people to deliver, to the best of our ability, an Afghanistan that is free, stable, prosperous and enjoying a dignified place in the region and the world." For the sake of Afghanistan, the region, and even the international community that must deal with the consequences of what happens in this often war-torn nation, much of the world hopes that this greatest of Karzai's dreams comes true.

TIMELINE

1957 Hamid Karzai is born in Kandahar, Afghanistan, on December 24.

1973 Sardar Mohammed Daoud Khan overthrows King Mohammad Zahir Shah in a bloodless coup.

1976–1982 Karzai attends Himachal University in Simla in Himachal Pradesh, India.

1977 Communist rebels overthrow Sardar Mohammed Daoud Khan.

1979 The Soviet Union invades Afghanistan to support its Communist government.

1989 The Soviet Union withdraws from Afghanistan after years of resistance from mujahideen; civil war begins.

1992 Karzai returns to Afghanistan and works as deputy foreign minister in the government of Burhanuddin Rabbani.

1994 Mullah Omar forms the Taliban.

1996 The Taliban exerts control over most of Afghanistan; Osama bin Laden moves to Afghanistan.

TIMELINE

1998 — Karzai marries. His wife, Zinat, is an obstetrician.

1999 — Karzai's father is murdered in Pakistan allegedly by a Taliban assassin.

2000 — Karzai warns the U.S. Senate Foreign Relations Committee about the Taliban.

2001 — Al Qaeda launches the 9/11 terrorist strikes in the United States; the United States invades Afghanistan; Karzai is selected and sworn in as interim president.

2002 — Karzai wins pledges of aid approaching $4 billion at an international donors conference in Japan; the United States incorporates and begins training soldiers for the Afghan National Army. Karzai escapes an assassination attempt.

2003 — A new Afghan constitution is drafted at a constitutional Loya Jirga.

2004 — Karzai wins democratic Afghanistan's first presidential election, escapes a second assassination attempt.

2005 — Afghanistan's first parliamentary election takes place.

2007 — The North Atlantic Treaty Organization (NATO) orders 12,000 troops to Afghanistan.

Glossary

Al Qaeda Literally, "the base," or "the foundation," an umbrella term for a network of terrorist organizations and cells widely believed to be responsible for the September 11, 2001, attacks on U.S. soil, among many other terrorist acts.

anarchy A state of disorder or lawlessness.

atheist A person who does not believe in a higher power or deity.

burka A traditional garment worn by women in Afghanistan and other Muslim nations that covers the wearer from head to toe. A mesh screen allows the wearer to see out of the garment; ostensibly worn to prevent males from viewing the woman's body.

CIA Central Intelligence Agency, the intelligence agency of the United States responsible for covert operations to secure American interests overseas.

Dari A dialect of the Persian language, and one of Afghanistan's two main languages, aside from Pashto.

financier One who provides money to a group, person, project, or cause.

guerrilla warfare A form of unconventional warfare where the attackers wage surprise attacks against often better-equipped or more numerous foes.

ISI Inter-Services Intelligence, the most powerful intelligence branch of the nation of Pakistan.

jihad From the Arabic word for struggle, this has come to mean "holy war" against an enemy; in many cases, an enemy of Islam.

mujahideen Most easily translated as "Muslims fighting in the Jihad," referring to soldiers of Islam fighting the foes of the religion.

mullah A religious leader or cleric of the Muslim faith.

Northern Alliance A union of primarily non-Pashtun Afghan minorities who helped fight and overthrow the Taliban.

Pashto The primary language spoken by Pashtuns.

Pashtuns The most numerous ethnic group of Afghanistan, comprising about 40 percent of the population.

sovereignty A nation's independence, politically and otherwise, from any other nation.

talib The Arabic word for student, or "seeker."

Taliban Islamic fundamentalist rulers of Afghanistan from 1996 to 2001. Overthrown by the U.S. and the Northern Alliance; literally means, "the students."

Uzbeks One of Afghanistan's minority groups, concentrated in the north; Uzbeks also have their own sovereign nation, Uzbekistan, which borders Afghanistan.

warlords Military commanders in many parts of Afghanistan that command their own armies, or militias, often working independently of the central government, or defying it altogether.

For More Information

Afghanistan Online
P.O. Box 11604
Pleasanton, CA 94588
Web site: http://www.afghan-web.com

The CIA World Factbook: Afghanistan
https://www.cia.gov/cia/publications/factbook/
    geos/af.html

The Consulate-General of Afghanistan
    in New York
360 Lexington Avenue, 11th Floor
New York, NY 10017
(212) 972-2276
(212) 972-2277
e-mail: afghancons@aol.com

The Embassy of Afghanistan
2341 Wyoming Avenue NW

Washington, DC 20008
(202) 483-6410
Web site: http://www.embassyofafghanistan.org

Revolutionary Association for the Women
of Afghanistan (RAWA)
P.O. Box 374
Quetta, Pakistan
e-mail: rawa@rawa.org
Web site: http://www.rawa.org

United States Department of State
2201 C Street NW
Washington, DC 20520
(202) 647-4000

WEB SITES

Due to the changing nature of Internet links,
Rosen Publishing has developed an online list of
Web sites related to the subject of this book.
This site is updated regularly. Please use this link
to access the list:

http://www.rosenlinks.com/nm/haka

For Further Reading

Greenblatt, Miriam. *Afghanistan: Enchantment of the World.* Danbury, CT: Children's Press, 2003.

Gunderson, Cory Gideon. *Afghanistan's Struggles* (World in Conflict—The Middle East). Edina, MN: ABDO & Daughters, 2003.

Otfinoski, Steven. *Afghanistan* (Nations in Transition). New York, NY: Facts on File, 2003.

Parks, Peggy. *Afghanistan* (Nations in Conflict). Chicago, IL: Blackbirch Press, 2003.

Streissguth, Thomas, ed. *Afghanistan* (History of Nations). Farmington Hills, MI: Greenhaven Press, 2005.

Todd, Anne M. *Hamid Karzai* (Major World Leaders). New York, NY: Chelsea House Publications, 2003.

Woodward, John, ed. *Afghanistan* (Opposing Viewpoints). Farmington Hills, MI: Greenhaven Press, 2006.

Bibliography

Akbar, Said Hyder. "Akbar at Yale: Warlords,
Econ, and John Adams." Slate.com.
November 15, 2005. Retrieved October
2006 (http://www.slate.com/id/2130424/
entry/2130425).

Associated Press. "NATO Attacks Taliban
Fighters Near Kabul." *New York Times*.
November 4, 2006.

BBC News. "Hamid Karzai: Shrewd Statesman."
BBC.com. June 14, 2002. Retrieved October
2006 (http://news.bbc.co.uk/2/hi/south_asia/
2043606.stm).

"Hamid Karzai Interview." Academy of
Achievement. June 7, 2002. Retrieved
October 2006 (http://www.achievement.org/
autodoc/page/kar0int-1).

"Interview: Lt. Colonel David Fox." Campaign
Against Terror. *Frontline*. September 8, 2002.
Retrieved October 2006 (http://www.pbs.org/

wgbh/pages/frontline/shows/campaign/
interviews/fox.html).

"Interview: President Hamid Karzai." Campaign
Against Terror. Frontline. September 8, 2002.
Retrieved October 2006 (http://www.pbs.org/
wgbh/pages/frontline/shows/campaign/inter-
views/karzai.html).

"Interview: U.S. Army Captain Jason Amerine."
Campaign Against Terror. *Frontline.* September 8,
2002. Retrieved October 2006 (http://
www.pbs.org/wgbh/pages/frontline/shows/
campaign/interviews/amerine.html).

Jones, Ann. "Letter from Afghanistan." *Nation.*
October 4, 2004.

Kamber, Michael. "Mujahideen Come Home: Things
Change and Remain the Same in Post-Taliban
Jalalabad." *Village Voice.* November 21–27, 2001.

Kaplan, Fred. "Knitting Together an Afghan
Strategy." Slate.com. June 20, 2006. Retrieved
October 2006 (http://www.slate.com/id/
2144094).

"Karzai Sworn in as Afghan Leader." CNN.com.
December 8, 2004. Retrieved October 2004

(http://www.cnn.com/2004/WORLD/asiapcf/
12/07/afghanistan.inauguration/index.html).

Kavanagh, Michael J. "Hamid Karzai and the
Hopeless 22." Slate.com. August 9, 2004.
Retrieved October 2006 (http://www.
slate.com/id/2104924).

Lyse, Doucet. "Afghanistan's Security Nightmare."
BBC News. January 8, 2004.

McGirk, Tim. "Sleeping in Mullah Omar's Bed."
Time. December 11, 2001. Retrieved October
2006 (http://www.time.com/time/columnist/
mcgirk/article/0,9565,188038,00.html).

"President Welcomes Afghan President Karzai
to the White House." Whitehouse.gov. May
23, 2005. Retrieved October 2006 (http://
www.whitehouse.gov/news/releases/2005/05/
20050523.html).

Rashid, Ahmed. *Taliban: Militant Islam, Oil and
Fundamentalism in Central Asia.* New Haven,
CT: Yale University Press, 2001.

Ratnesar, Romesh, and Aryn Baker. "Interview with
Hamid Karzai." *Time.* September 10, 2006.
Retrieved October 2006 (http://

www.time.com/time/magazine/article/
0,9171,1533452,00.html).

Reuters. "Karzai Ventures into Afghan Streets."
November 2, 2006.

Rohde, David. "Afghan Symbol for Change
Becomes a Symbol of Failure." *New York
Times.* September 5, 2006.

Rohde, David, and James Risen. "C.I.A. Review
Highlights Afghan Leader's Woes." *New York
Times.* November 5, 2006.

Wafa, Abdul Waheed. "70 Taliban Killed in
Night Battle, NATO Force Says." *New York
Times.* October 30, 2006.

Index

ABOUT THE AUTHOR

Philip Wolny is a writer, editor, and novelist. Born in Bydgoszcz, Poland, at the height of the Cold War, he immigrated to the United States with his parents at the age of four. He graduated from Stony Brook University in New York. He is currently earning a master's degree in Euroculture at Jagiellonian University in Krakow, Poland.

PHOTO CREDITS

Cover (background) © Prakash Singh/AFP/Getty Images; cover (foreground), pp. 5, 76 © Paula Bronstein/Getty Images; p. 13 © Imagno/Contributor/Getty Images; pp. 16, 95 © AP/Wide World Photos; p. 19 © Getty Images; p. 25 © AFP/AFP/Getty Images; p. 31 © Magnum/Abbas; p. 33 © Getty Images; p. 34 © Emmanuel Dunand/AFP/Getty Images; pp. 39, 42 © AFP/Getty Images; p. 49 © Sion Touhig/Getty Images; p. 55 © Chris Hondros/Getty Images; p. 58 © Jimin Lai/AFP/Getty Images; p. 63 © Shah Marai/AFP/Getty Images; p. 71 © Banaras Khan/AFP/Getty Images; pp. 73, 88 © Mark Wilson/Getty Images; p. 79 © Liu Jin/AFP/Getty Images; p. 82 © John Moore/Getty Images; p. 85 © John D. McHugh/AFP/Getty Images; p. 93 © Mandel Ngan/AFP/Getty Images.

Designer: Gene Mollica; **Editor:** Wayne Anderson